Elegant Leaders Advantage

LEAD WITH INFLUENCE TO IMPACT

From the author of

7 Steps to Become an Elegant Leader with Voltage

and

Step in the Boat, a lifelong journey of purpose

This workbook is a guide with takeaways from the Elegant Leader with Voltage system. You will learn how to apply the takeaways from these personalized sessions into your own life.

JScott Partners Publishing
ALPHARETTA, GEORGIA

JScott Partners, Inc.
5174 McGinnis Ferry Rd
Alpharetta, GA 30005
www.brookestoneassociates.com

Layout: Joel Friedlander

Ordering Information:
Quantity sales. Special discounts are available on quantity purchases by corporations, associations, and others. For details, contact the "Special Sales" at the web or physical address above

Elegant Leaders Advantage – a guidebook to Influence with Impact/ J. Scott Spector. —1st ed.
ISBN 978-1-0735147-8-6

Contents

Orientation Meeting

Prior to your first session, you will receive the following:

- ***Participant Agreement***

- ***My Commitment***

- ***Elegant Leaders Blueprint***

- ***Feedback Guidelines***

This meeting is held via conference call or online web conference.

Participant Agreement

I, _____, agree:

1. I will be present for and participate in all sessions.

2. I will be on time and stay for all sessions.

3. I will complete the program.

4. Everything said and shared in this group is confidential. I will not share anything said with anyone outside this group.

5. I will be open, honest, constructive, respectful and professional.

6. I will be positive in my communications. If I have a complaint, I will frame it in the form of a constructive and positive request.

7. I am open and willing to hear advice and receive coaching.

8. I will make the group a safe place where people can say what is on their minds.

My Commitment

1. My commitment is to your professional and organizational success.
2. I will be fully prepared ensuring your sessions are time well spent.
3. I will be available and supportive as your coach, including between meetings as needed.
4. I will be open, honest, constructive, respectful and professional.
5. I am open to your feedback on how to bring greater value to your experience in this program.

What questions do you have about my agreement with you?

What requests do you have in addition to what I have stated here?

My commitment is 100% to your success during this program and beyond. I am accessible between meetings as needed. I want you to be comfortable reaching out to me with questions or as a sounding board any time. If I can do anything to make your experience in this program more valuable, let me know.

Elegant Leaders Blueprint

AREA	FOR YOUR CAREER	FOR YOUR ORGANIZATION OR AREA OF RESPONSIBILITY
VISION		
MISSION		
VALUES		
EDGE		
KEY PERFORMANCE INDICATORS		
TOP 3 INITIATIVES		
PROFESSIONAL RELATIONSHIPS		
DEVELOPMENT		
RECONCILIATION		

www.elegantleader.net

Treat Feedback as a Gift

All of us want to know we're performing to our potential. Positive feedback is generally more well received than negative feedback. I can recall the days when I received a "poop sandwich." Someone you work with or for tells you, "...you did a great job, but..." You immediately forget everything that was said prior to the but and frankly you think the person who imparted their feedback on you is a butt.

However, we all need clear and concise feedback on what went _____,

what didn't and what _____ we have learned. It's important to be prepared in

case you need to hear things you weren't expecting to hear. Here's what's important to remember:

1. Treat feedback as a _____. Be grateful. People are giving you advice and counsel about how to be more successful.

2. Your role is not your _____. Often, we confuse our role in an organization with who we are as a person. You are not your job so there's no need to get defensive. Feedback is about role performance.

3. It's not about _____ or

    _____. It's about receiving data and not an argument or an

    emotional event. Relax.

4. Direct the advice so it _____ you. Ask for specific examples to understand what their basis is and what they're trying to tell you. It's not to debate or argue. You're listening for specific behaviors, attitudes and metrics to help you become more successful. Ask, what would you like to see instead of what they are seeing

5. Where appropriate, make _____. Apologize and commit to being better.

Preface

Elegant Leadership with Voltage does not comprise luck, goal setting or merely execution. Elegant Leaders execute plans with emotional intelligence and a clear, concise and compelling message of dedication and resolve to persevere regardless of circumstances seen and unseen. The leader who subscribes to everything in this world happens by a complex mechanism of cause and effect is reactive and weak. The questions become:

- Do you have the **Ability**, **Balance** and **Control** to perform at an Elite level?
- Is there a combination of **Inherent Characteristics** and **Learned Skills**?
- Is there a **Desire** for the responsibilities, challenges and opportunities required by senior-level roles?
- Does the leader have emotional and cogent **Commitment**, effort and intent to **Persevere** when times get tough?

Let's define an Elegant Leader with Voltage:

Elegance is dignified, graceful, refined and polished.

Leadership is guiding, inspiring, showing direction, serving, listening and learning. When putting the adjective and noun together, what appears is an inspirational model to guide and serve people, teams, families and organizations in a simple, powerful, practical and graceful manner.

Why lead elegantly?

What separates the poor from the good and the great leader? How should a leader look to others and how should they behave? Is it okay to coerce people to get the results necessary? Conversely, is it okay to have such an inviting and amiable environment providing minimal results? And finally, what role does ego play with relationships and results? There's not one of us who doesn't have areas in which we need to grow. Remember the "L" in Leadership, every Elegant Leader with Voltage must master: *"Be a good listener and a lifelong learner."*

Becoming an Elegant Leader means the whole is better than its parts - the results prove without their leadership a considerably healthier future of the enterprise wouldn't exist. An Elegant Leader is challenged with understanding how to find freedom, discover your purpose and make a difference in everyone's life. This working book is a practical guide to leadership while providing reference to works that form the foundation for the practice of leadership. Elegant Leadership happens anytime we influence the thinking, behaviors and/or the development of another person. It's our duty, responsibility and calling to Lead Elegantly with Voltage!

Elegant Leadership with Voltage is grounded in the rhythm between Ego, Results and Relationships. They are all intertwined. The space where the three circles intersect is the enabling power and spiritual healing - Grace - required to Lead Elegantly.

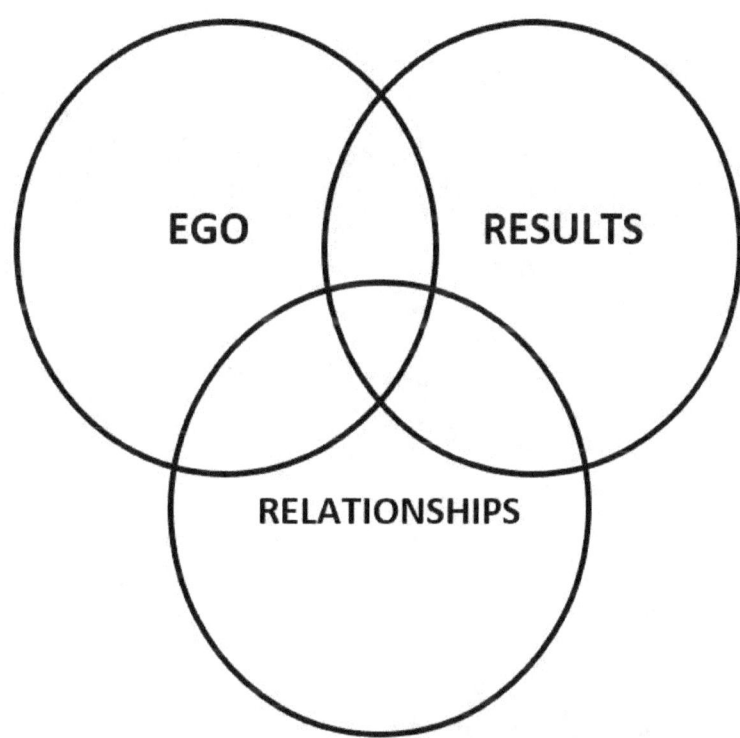

Before you dive in, pause for a moment and think about the people who have most influenced your thinking, behaviors and your life's journey. As their names return to you, their roles and organization are just a part of the overall leadership landscape. Let's take what you do well and perfect it! This book is nothing more than a tool, a resource, a method for you to adopt, personalize it and make it your own. If you cannot answer these 3 questions immediately, then this book is for you.

Are you prepared for the realities of today filled with the uncertainty of tomorrow?

Where are you looking to anticipate the next change?

Are you courageous enough to abandon the past results for a direction that may be unfamiliar or uncomfortable?

CHAPTER 1

Getting Comfortable in Your Own Skin

The longest relationship we will ever have is with ourselves. You've been with yourself for a very long time and habits are hard to change. What is it costing you? At some point in our lives, we become increasingly self-conscious and dependent on how others perceive us. What you are on the inside is a direct reflection on the outside. Who are you projecting and how is that reflection dependent or influenced by who you are interacting with?

Become aware of behaviors you want to change. It takes thick skin to ask for feedback on behaviors that can be damaging your relationships and your performance.

Set goals for new behaviors. Now that the veil has been removed on your behaviors, it is time to clearly state what you will do to change your negative behaviors, how you'll change them, by when, how will you measure the change and what new behaviors you will adopt.

Seek counsel and eliminate past mistakes. If you make it to this point, then you have passed over 65% of those that began this process and have demonstrated great courage. Getting advice on both effective and ineffective behaviors could be priceless to you and your career. Admit your mistakes, clear up any resentment and poor relationships now.

Track your improvement and follow up. Behaviors are like seasonal crops – they're cultivated over many years – don't expect them to change overnight, because you want them to. Habits are hard to break, and at the first sign of stress, we're likely to revert to our bad behaviors. We're going to teach you and show you how to respond.

Elegant Leaders successfully navigate the rhythm of three tensions: satisfying their Ego, achieving Results and building powerful Relationships. Our egos represent a healthy sense of self, joy from our success, status, prestige and so on. Some gurus believe all ego is bad. We take a more rhythmic approach because we all tend to move from healthy egos and based on our behaviors move towards unhealthy egos. Too strong an ego will sacrifice results and relationships.

Ironically, the best way to satisfy ego is to build strong relationships and working diligently to get solid results. When results and relationships are in place, a healthy ego follows along naturally. There are many signs of an unhealthy ego. The following self-assessment presents a few ways for you to 'self-diagnose' where you are today. If you check no to any of the questions, you have an opportunity to adjust or avoid those behaviors and substitute a healthier alternative.

Does Your Ego Get In The Way?

	Yes	No
I look for opportunities for people to take over my role so I can do more challenging things.		
I seek out ways to share credit with others		
I take risks, even when the outcome may make me look less than favorable		
If my colleagues or peers were asked, my ego does not get in the way and success doesn't go to my head		
Salary, titles, corner office and things are important to me. However, what's most rewarding is serving those I lead and getting them to reach or exceed their potential		
I make decisions based on getting results and keeping strong relationships. Personal gain is a by-product of the first two.		
I don't claim to have or know all the answers and seek out differing perspectives		

Notes and Observations:

We all live and die by the results we achieve. Some of our success comes from proper goal setting, execution, repeating proven disciplines, and holding people accountable to achieve certain outcomes. However, when we sacrifice relationships at the cost of achieving those results, those relationships will not be long-lasting. You'll get compliance and as a result you'll also get resentment. This assessment presents a few ways to tell if you're solely focused on results.

Do You Overemphasize Results?

	Yes	No
I want and frankly demand results, but I will not raise my voice or berate anyone		
When I work with people on projects, I try hard to help others personally and professionally.		
I sometimes have to apply pressure and I do that judiciously to the situation.		
Many of my former colleagues and peers have asked us to work together on other projects or to join them in other companies or ventures.		
I always ask myself, 'am I getting results' and 'am I preserving or strengthening this(these) relationship(s)'		
I make decisions based on getting results and keeping strong relationships. I won't sacrifice one over the other.		
I'm not looking to sacrifice people to get the results I must have. I work hard to find their aspirations, so we all win in the end.		

Notes and Observations:

Leaders invest both time and energy in building, strengthening, preserving and repairing relationships. However, as with ego and results, overemphasizing relationships can cause problems. When there's too much focus on relationships where results are sacrificed, nothing gets done and eventually people lose their respect. Leaders lose relationships because of negotiated standards and lack of accountability. Take the following assessment and think about ways to improve your rhythm between ego, results and relationships.

Are You Overemphasizing Relationships?

	Yes	No
Conflict can sometimes be quite healthy, and I encourage dialog and respect differences		
I understand the differences between being popular or respected. I prefer to be respected.		
I sometimes have to replace people on my team if they're ineffective; regardless whether they're liked or a friend.		
I often think about strengthening key relationships while getting the results we must have.		
Situations can get tense and when they do, I assert myself appropriately. I don't avoid conflict to protect a relationship.		
I am comfortable with dissenting opinions in our meetings even when it creates conflict. I'm not trying to mediate or bring harmony to avoid productive dialog.		

Notes and Observations:

The 3 things I'm comfortably committed to working on over the next 30 days – especially under pressure – to bring Ego, Results and Relationships in a better rhythm are:

Are You Comfortable in the Gray?

How do you react in time of uncertainty and ambiguity?

- ◯ I tend to overreact and panic under pressure
- ◯ I prefer to act swiftly on my own instead of waiting and exploring with other
- ◯ I like sure things and resist uncertainty and change when there's no options
- ◯ I like uncertainty, forging new territory and I encourage others to experiment
- ◯ I like adventure and sometimes go out on a limb, maybe when i don't need to.

Leading through uncertainty and ambiguity can be uncomfortable and even scary for some. Those who persist in the face of risk almost always reap great rewards. To do that, leaders must step out from where it's comfortable and walk through what's uncomfortable – learn from failure, remain calm under pressure and turn any setback into a comeback. One of the most essential elements of becoming an Elegant Leader with Voltage is knowing yourself enough to be comfortable in the gray – the area of uncertainty and ambiguity – and to trust your performance.

Additional Resources:

The Elegant Leader with Voltage platform has been developed over two decades of proven-in-the-field principles and fine-tuned with every project. There are over twenty-five toolkits offered to improve job performance, increase the communication and engagement with your team and create a healthier work-life rhythm. Leaders who would benefit from Getting Comfortable in Your Own Skin framework, may also benefit from:

Behavioral and Perceptual Coaching – how behaviors follow attitudes; how reframing limiting beliefs is a gamechanger. There are many ways to make the new belief a habit. Here, the Behavioral Coaching framework and Perceptual Coaching framework become almost identical and are integral in evolving the proper disciplines required to Lead Elegantly with great results and stronger relationships.

Leading Change – with the right attitudes it's easier to lead change, do what needs to be done and make difficult decisions. Here's how you can effortlessly generate peak performance in your role as the leader. The dirty little secret is we don't always feel like leading – some days we just need a break, a time-out from giving to everyone else. It takes tremendous energy to muster the resilience to lead, especially in the face of ongoing volatility, organizational friction, and setbacks

Create a High-Performance Growth Culture – together we start with you and how you are the one to model the desired culture before creating the culture for others, like a chocolate fountain. We help you get your organization to the root cause of achieving higher performance. Stop tolerating organizational performance that's not meeting your expectations. Everything changes in the way your people and teams communicate, get things done, and achieve results with us.

Succession Planning - as more and more baby boomers retire; succession planning is a critical stage for ever-evolving organizations. A key component is uncovering the wealth that's trapped in a business you've grown and nurtured over the years. You have options – family or 3rd party transition or preparing for a suitable buyer to sell and exit - we've been working with businesses from $5-10M to multi-unit closely-held generational companies to $50M for over fifteen years. We understand the family dynamics and dysfunction that comes with this season of life. We walk you through exactly how to assess, design and implement a robust succession plan.

Notes:

Notes:

CHAPTER 2

Communicating Simply and Powerfully

This entire guidebook is about communication! From finding the right process that works for you, establishing an Elegant Strategy, strengthening relationships, staying grounded and gaining clarity, to moving things forward to influence and impact people Elegant Leaders communicate simply and powerfully. Some of you have received coaching and guidance on communication. You understand over 90% of communication is non-verbal, so you pay attention to your tone and body language when you show up as the leader. You understand how to listen to other people's emotions and not just their words. You take into account people's motives and intentions. Finally, you know people interpret what they hear through numerous filters, thus communication takes precision.

The Elegant Leaders Advantage is about communication and many of you know how to communicate effectively, or do you? There are five critical themes involving communicating simply and powerfully people sometimes forget. You can Be the Message and have your actions speak more clearly and concisely than your words. You can Be Authentic and speak truth in a way that enables results and strengthens relationships, and you can listen with purpose and generosity while being emotionally intelligent. Elegant Leaders change how they listen based on their situation. Elegant Leaders synthesize information into simple, powerful statements enabling people to remember more easily and respond positively.

Our focus today will be on treating communication as a critical process. Take a look at your organization. Communicating as a system must be taken as serious as marketing, payables/receivables, manufacturing operations and sales. Elegant Leaders design both formal and informal communication networks ensuring everyone receives consistent, relevant information. Sounds simple, doesn't it? Sadly, it's one of the most overlooked and thus misinterpreted vehicles of an organization. Elegant Leaders over communicate with everyone – there is no guesswork. It's a critical process of their personal and professional persona.

There are numerous ways to communicate to people – from informally walking around to distributing corporate-wide memos. Whether you're solving complex problems or announcing celebrations, some begin at the top of an organization and some originate from the front lines, communicating as a system cascades through an organization via formal and informal networks. Follow the chart below and then answer questions from your company experience:

Communication Vehicles and Content

Vehicle	Purpose	Message, for instance
Town-hall meetings	Goals and strategy	Goals
Management meetings	Share information	Budget
Off-site retreats	Engagement	Vision
One-on-one's	Seek advice	Mission
Intranet site	Two-way dialog	Strategy
Newsletter	Brainstorm	Knowledge
Pay stub insert	Collaborate	Protocols
Formal reports	Socialize	Norms
Memos	Learn and develop	Expectations
Lunch'n learn	Apply pressure	Behaviors

NOTE: do not read the chart left to right thinking this is the vehicle and then it's associated purpose and what gets communicated. The above is a specific list on vehicles, purposes and messages.

What key groups or key people need to be communicating more effectively together? How can you facilitate communication within these people or groups? What could drive improved communications?

What messages does your organization communicate very well? How about poorly? How can you address the weaker areas? What are you willing to do to improve the system?

What impact would be being more available and accessible to your people to engage in dialog with them?

How can you facilitate improved communications within your organization? How can you help others improve relationships with one another? Are there internal boundaries needing to be broken or blown up?

What 3 things must you do to be successful in your role or function?

What 3 things any new member to your organization must do to be successful?

Listen to Listen – without fixing, interrupting or judging
Listen to understand their interests and aspirations
Listen for an opportunity to move the organization forward
Listen to serve, and Listen to impact someone else's life

Your **TWO BONUSES** are on the next two pages. The *7 Levels of Communication* and *4 Methods to Resolve Conflict*. Let's review how to apply them to any situation.

7 Levels of Communication

Superficial Communications

Most of your communications are on the surface
Social Media, Water cooler conversations
Some non-verbal communications

General Communications

Gathering and sharing data
Passing information off as 'need to know'
The 411, 611, 911 messaging

Deep Feelings

This is where real meaningful communication occurs, may need validation
Is environment safe? Is there conflict? 'When this happens, it makes me feel...'
What consequences exist? What recrimination happens as a result?

Deep Needs

Successful managers and leaders understand the deepest needs of their people
Why do we not know? Why do we have this issue?
Barriers to Communication – withdrawal, escalation and more

Truth

Be gracious and grateful; say thank you
Openly express yourself
Be encouraging

Kindness

What have you done to support and reinforce the environment?

Get Comfortable in the Uncomfortable

4 Methods to Resolve Conflict

Respond v React   *Decisions are not emotional*

Resolving conflict is a choice. Make some pre-decisions by making pre-conflict rules

It's okay to be angry. It's not okay to be hateful

Solve it now! Don't wait to put it off – get it done!

No name calling – that's not who you are. Avoid raising your voice – harsh words stir up anger.

Avoid getting historical and hysterical. Be specific instead of saying 'always' or 'never'

Focus on Positives   *You're not going to change them until you change you*

Change you by Being the Leader you're called to be

If not, then find another role you're better suited for

Do whatever is true, noble, right and admirable. Find it!

Stop the We v. They   *Extend your leadership to others*

It's not up to you to take revenge

Can't put out a fire with fire so stop trying

You can't resolve it if you think you can't

Improve Capacity Towards Others   *Lend a hand*

Who helped you get to where you are?

What have you done to get others to where you are?

Have you been the leader you're meant to be or are you asleep at the wheel?

Notes:

_____

Notes:

CHAPTER 3

Engage and Mobilize People

This chapter focuses on the most important relationships you have. It's likely you've worked in or lived through work situations in various industries and sectors, and you've worked for some characters who were, let's just say less, than honorable or worthy of their title. It's easy to come away from those experiences wondering if there's anyone worthy enough to lead, inspire and mobilize people. When you're exposed to many different organizations, you learn examples of great and not-so great leadership. Here we'll describe a simple, graceful way to lead and mobilize people using two of eight strategies. They are:

Get to Know Your Employees
Develop Messages that Engage and Mobilize
Earn the Right to Advance
Set Clear Expectations and
Personalize Your Leadership
Recognize and Acknowledge Everyone
Develop People for the Future
Seek Advice to Improve Your Lead

This series is going to focus on two of the most vital areas of engaging and mobilizing your people – knowing your people and earning the right to advance. There are five critical aspects you must know and be authentic about each of your direct reports, colleagues, volunteers or family members. You must discover what are their aspirations and goals, what behaviors and principles are most important, what gifts and talents do they possess, how do they learn best and how far can they go in your organization – not how far you think they can go. The next page gives you a blank template to 'figure that out.' How? Ask them deep, powerful questions. Get to know them! Build a relationship.

Name:

_____

Worksheet: Get to Know Me

Convictions	
Values	
Gifts	
Style	
Career Trajectory	
What else?	

Notes:

Your position, rank or title doesn't guarantee you any right to lead whatsoever. In fact, it's more of a hindrance because of the invisible barriers to authority that are perpetuated. An Elegant Leader is charged with being competent, credible, committed and with high character. These attributes help you earn the right to advance with people to serve them. Take this self-assessment and then give it to your peers and your directs for their impression of you. It takes courage to lead and courage to have objective feedback.

Worksheet: Earn Your Right To Advance

People would say this about me:	Strongly Agree	Agree	Unsure	Disagree	Strongly Disagree
I am competent – my expertise helps people getting them the resources they need and offer guidance. I model right behaviors					
I am credible – my track record speaks to results					
I am committed – people know I'm committed to their development and success and that of the organization					
I am of good character – people trust me and trust me to do what's right, to keep my word and to model the right principles					
I am human – my willingness to admit mistakes comes naturally. I ask for help when needed and have a balanced sense of humor. We get it done as a team, even if it means being vulnerable					
I am resilient – I'm comfortable with major setbacks, extreme pressure and can remain calm in most situations. I am a source of strength and find a way to have a comeback					
I serve others – I look for ways to serve the interests of my people and their/our commitments.					

Based on your findings, what is one area you see a need to improve?

What actions can you take and what actions are you willing to take?

My One Area of Improvement:

What behaviors can you begin to change today? What attitudes can you begin to shift to improve?

Specific people I work with frequently from whom I need to earn the right to advance and lead:

One behavior I can change immediately:

One attitude I can change immediately:

Now that you've addressed some immediate needs to engage and mobilize your people, where do you think things went off track?

If you hadn't registered for this series, what do you think would have happened had you not changed anything?

If you're not clear or successful this time, what do you think will happen?

SPECIAL BONUS:

---

8 Messages to Engage and Mobilize

An Elegant Leader must understand the factors for driving engagement and to create and implement a clear plan to improve those factors. Here's how you can create a plan with each person, how-to implement your plan and drive engagement with Voltage.

Dimension	Your Message
History	Share where we've been and what we've achieved. What needs to be cleared up before moving on? What do we need to acknowledge and celebrate?"
Vision / Mission	Here's where we're going, and how would you build upon it? Here's why we're doing this. Is it compelling enough for you to contribute at and above your potential? What do you see us working toward?
Values	Here are the principles we hold dear here. Here's how I like us to be. How do these values fit within your own personal values?
Strategies / Tactics	In general, this is how we're planning to get there. You were hired because you bring a certain 'how' and I need your help to figure out what that looks like in your area of accountability.
Objectives	Here are the specific metrics we define performance by. Here are the specific measurements we will achieve for every dimension – internal, external and other constituents.
Commitment	Why are you here? What are your aspirations? How does your commitment fit with the dimensions listed above?
Roles / Goals	Here is what I want you to achieve. Here's why it's important to all the above listed dimensions.
Support	What do you need form me to be successful? What resources will you need to be successful? What else can I do to facilitate your success?

Notes:

CHAPTER 4

Influence with Impact

To lead elegantly, you must be able to influence people to act, feel, speak and think differently. Without this skill you will not get results or create positive change through anyone. It is both art and science. Science because certain principles apply in any influence situation – certain strategies, certain behaviors prove time and again to be effective. Influence is an art; reading people, thinking creatively and comprehensively and responding instantaneously to someone's concerns and issues.

We will discuss a simply, powerful approach to help you hone the scientific side of influence. We will look at an overview of the principle drivers of successful influence, a proven process to follow and a set of tools to identify the correct strategy and associated tactics. We will cover two principles of influence that enable influence, critical assessment of situations as the more you know about another person's motivations as well as your own, and how to choose the most appropriate appeal to the other person to achieve your influence goal.

Principle #1 – People Do Things for Their Reasons, Not Yours.

The key to influencing another person is to connect what you want with reasons, possibilities, interests, and commitments that matter to them, not you. If you want a colleague to join you for Italian food, you can talk about your favorite Italian restaurants. So, who cares? What's the probability of influencing them to join you if you talk about things that matter to them or their interest in trying new things, their love of homemade dishes centuries old or their desire to relax in the warm environs of the Italian clientele? A secret to principle one is most leaders need to be reminded of this principle often! How do we get there? Set a goal by asking explicitly what you must have.

Principle #2 – Influence Happens One Person at a Time.

You can't influence the government, the company, the Board, or the committee of "them." However, you can influence Senator Bob White, the Vice-President of Sales, or the Chairman of the Executive committee. Influence happens person-by-person, one conversation by one conversation.

First Things First

The first principle of influence is people do things for their reasons, not for your reasons. By assessing a situation ahead of time, you increase your chances of identifying the other person's reasons. From here you can then prepare a strategy that helps the other person get what he or she wants, while you get what you want. You'll also learn about yourself and where you'll flex and where you won't.

The worksheet provided is a simple framework for assessing a situation. It starts by challenging you to understand the other person's motivations, interests and intentions. It then asks about your own positions and interests. Using this worksheet ahead of time, you can develop a strong strategy and increase your chances of success during your actual influence situation.

Worksheet: Assess the Situation

What will inspire them in this situation?	
What reasons might influence them? What benefits does this person receive by changing? What do they give up by not changing?	
What incentive can you provide that they would value?	
What are their primary interests and concerns and how can you respect their concerns?	
How can you address their issues before bringing up your own?	
Where are you willing to be open to their ideas? Where are you not willing to be flexible?	

Let's Be Specific

Influence another person begins with a specific, measurable goal. Without a goal, you won't know where you're headed, if you'll get there or not. Without a goal, how would you develop a plan or an approach for a desired result you want to achieve? Most leaders set out to influence people without a goal at al. Let's look at examples of good and bad – ineffective and effective goals.

Vague Goal	*Effective Influence Goal*
Sally will agree to be more involved in my project	Sally will agree to spend two hours a week on my project, dedicate one full time staff person and attend the weekly update meeting. She will begin next Tuesday.
Jim and I will work together to generate more grant funding	Jim will agree to secure at least eight grant and foundation sources by next month. Together, we will provide all necessary documentation to complete the grant requirements over the next six weeks. As long as I can show Jim how we are on time, he will agree to devote more time to this initiative.
Dana will be more supportive of my work	Dana will agree to present a precis of my unit's strategy to her staff at next Wednesday's meeting. She will publicly state, at this meeting, her support of our initiative I'm leading to improve our quality and service.

Think about a situation where you must influence someone to achieve results you must have. Who will you attempt to influence? What influence goal will tell you whether you succeeded?

Person to be Influenced:

Worksheet: Set the Table

What must this person do differently?	
What do you want them to do or to say?	
What would you like them to think?	
What would you like them to feel?	
By when?	

Four Domains of Elegant Leadership

The Four Domains of Elegant Leadership with Voltage require you and your lead to be in proper order. We've been taught all our lives to lead with our knowledge, skills and abilities. Those attributes are not sustainable if your heart is in the wrong place – you're leading with improper motives or intentions. There's a natural order of things and there's a natural order to true and proper leadership that is long lasting even after you've left an organization.

Heart. Your leadership influences other people's thinking and behaviors. It's up to you to decide whether you will act out of self-interest or on behalf of those you lead. Elegant Leadership with Voltage forces you to make a change from the inside. Your 'why' or purpose greater than self is found. Leading with your heart is difficult and exposes you for who you really are. Are you prepared to be vulnerable? This core value of your life influences everything you say and do as a leader and enables you to stand up when everything else around you falls apart. The space where the three concentric circles – ego, results and relationships - are intertwined is grace as your source.

Head. The heart guides your motivation and your head determines your beliefs and theories about leading and inspiring people. Your leadership philosophy and your attitudes on influence guide how you emphasize your point of view. Your lead is to serve others. If you don't get the heart right, you won't have the capacity to lead effectively towards the results you must have while maintaining strong healthy relationships. Your good intentions travel to your head when the heart is on target.

Hands. You demonstrate what's in your heart and head by what you do with your hands. The hands of an Elegant Leader with Voltage are comfortable with raw materials – *people* – assessing both the current state and future potential. Hands invest in people and consider the cost before the work begins.

There's a carefully defined plan on how the hands are to be utilized to transform, inspire, and equip people to go forth. Elegant Leaders are master craftsman because of their expertise with the tools of the trade. Elegant Leaders are happiest when those they lead can carry on without us and continue the work that was begun before them.

Habits. These are the activities you do to stay focused on the promise inside the process. There are habits you 'are' and habits you 'do'. To have a successful rhythm between being and doing takes energy, focus and perspective. When you establish an environment of safety trust emerges! Innovation, creativity and work becomes fun and exciting instead of fear, dread and loathing. Remember, you can extend forgiveness without excusing an act done against you; however, you have to be willing to submit your own ego to Lead Elegantly.

Do you want to have better influence with people and be able to impact the work they do and the person they are? Make sure your motives and intentions are honorable. Take the self-assessment below and get your domains in order.

Worksheet: Improving What Lies Beneath

What's becomes possible by changing my behaviors, perceptions and habits for my career and organization?	
What 3 strengths can I build upon?	
What attitudes and behaviors are holding me and my career back?	
What positive behaviors do I need to start or do more of?	
What becomes possible by affecting how I'm perceived in improving and building on healthy behaviors?	
What ONE behavior are you committing to STOP?	
Who can you count on to be an ally in keeping you accountable to your commitment?	
Who are you willing to speak with, get honest feedback from, admit your mistakes and make amends?	
How will you measure success and track your results?	

Notes:

Appendix

The Elegant Leader Blueprint

Our first step in the 7 Steps to Become an Elegant Leader with Voltage is starting with you personalized Blueprint. You can get your complementary Blueprint by going to https://tinyurl.com/23ctcrn3 There are additional insights on how to apply the proven principles daily.

Communicate Simply and Powerfully

Leadership presence is a huge topic today and getting to the heart of having true leadership presence in every kind of communication is what this framework is about simply and powerfully. Discover what it means to be an effective communicator and think strategically about communication as an important process in an organization. To go deeper visit: https://brookestoneassociates.com/leadership/csp/

Engage and Mobilize Employees

Leaders often struggle with what they can do to have a more cohesive, engaged and productive group of employees. The billion-dollar costs of this situation are staggering in terms of employee turnover, low productivity, decreased customer satisfaction, the potential for increased error rates, and more. We deliver a six-step process that bakes in a comprehensive leadership and talent development process here: https://brookestoneassociates.com/leadership/engage/

About the Author

J. Scott Spector, a native of Richmond, Virginia, is *The Culture Whisperer* - an executive with over 25 years of experience in organizational development, corporate turnarounds and change management. He has worked with hundreds of CEO's as a leadership advisor, strategist and executive coach in over 12 countries. He has developed numerous leadership pipelines in a variety of fields, including, health care, manufacturing and distribution, professional services and non-profits.

Scott inspires leaders and businesses to inspire their people when they struggle with moving things forward in their organization, setting strategic direction, engaging and mobilizing employees, and creating a high-performance growth culture. As an entrepreneur owning and operating highly profitable businesses through sale and exit, he's honed his real-world expertise by navigating today's landmines and tomorrow's emerging marketplace.

He received his MBA from the Pamplin School of Business at Virginia Polytechnic and State University in Blacksburg, Virginia. In 2017, he earned his Professional Coaching Certificate from the International Coaching Federation. He currently resides in Alpharetta, Georgia, and has two grown children, and when he's not helping people lead elegantly, you can find him playing golf.

Best wishes,